MASS
IN
TIME
OF
WAR

(PAUKENMESSE)

FOR FOUR-PART CHORUS OF MIXED VOICES
AND SOLOS WITH PIANO ACCOMPANIMENT

Edited by

MICHAEL R. MILLER

ED2600

G. SCHIRMER, *Inc.*

DISTRIBUTED BY

HAL•LEONARD®
CORPORATION

7777 W. BLUEMOUND RD. P.O. BOX 13819 MILWAUKEE, WI 53213

Preface

Unlike some of Haydn's other works, the title of this mass comes from Haydn himself. He termed it *Missa in Tempore Belli,* and dated it 1796. At this time Austria was waging a losing war against France as Napoleon, then a young general, continued to win every battle. In August of 1796 the government in Vienna, under the Emperor Franz, proclaimed general mobilization and forbade any discussion of peace until the French were driven from Austria. At this time, Haydn was probably working on the "Agnus Dei." His use of prominent timpani passages suggests distant cannon fire and the trumpet fanfares have a definite military character. The closing section, "Dona Nobis Pacem," is not only a prayer for peace but for victory.

According to H. C. R. Landon, there are two authentic orchestrations of this work. The latter one, which has been used as the basis of this piano reduction, includes pairs of oboes, clarinets, bassoons, horns and trumpets, timpani, strings, organ continuo, and a flute solo in the "Qui Tollis" of the "Gloria." It was used in a performance in Vienna, December 26, 1796.

The earlier version, used at the first performance in Eisenstadt on September 13 of that year, omits the horns completely and also the clarinets, except in the "Credo," and has no flute solo.

All tempi, dynamics, and phrasing are strictly from original sources. However, as this is intended to be a practical edition, ornaments such as turns (∾) and *appoggiature* (originally in small notes) have been written out to avoid ambiguities in rhythm.

M. R. M.

Mass in Time of War
(Paukenmesse)

Kyrie

Joseph Haydn (1732-1809)
Edited by Michael R. Miller

45723cX

Allegro moderato

SOPRANO SOLO

Ky - ri - e____ e - lei - son, e - lei - son,

Ky - ri - e e - lei - son, e - lei - - son, e - lei - - son,

Ky - ri - e_____ e - lei -

4

Gloria

20

30

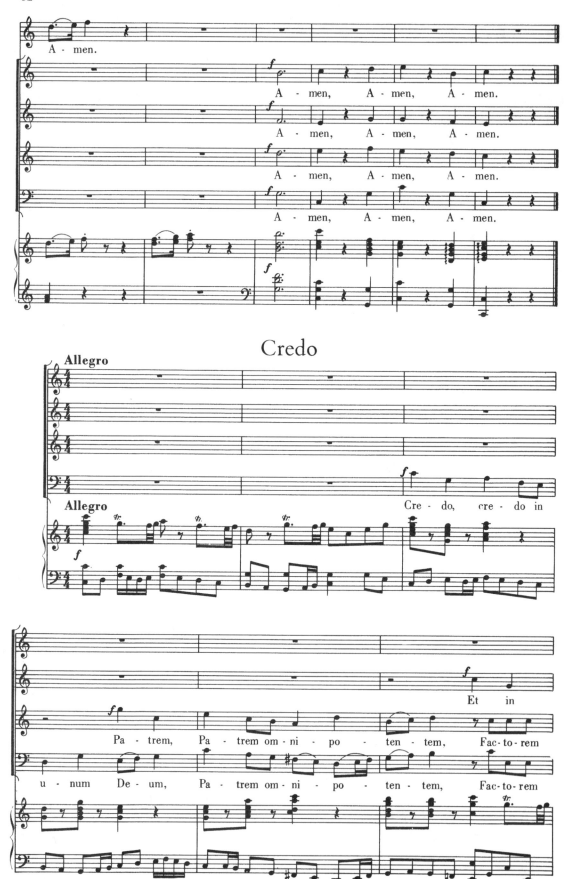

32

Credo

45723

40

45723

46

45723

52

45723

Sanctus

Benedictus

60

45723

Agnus Dei